Forgetting Ted Hughes

by Jane Cassady

The Pale Ale Poets Series

*Dedicated to Rachel Kinney,
in eternal, abstract friendship.*

**FarStarFire Press
August 2000**

www.FarStarFire.com

Forgetting Ted Hughes

Copyright © 2000 Jane Cassady
All Rights Reserved

Consulting Editors:

> John Gardiner
> John C. Harrell
> Lee Mallory

Printed in The United States of America

by

FarStarFire Press
26701 Quail Creek, Suite 251
Laguna Hills, CA 92656
949.362.7499
www.FarStarFire.com
info@FarStarFire.com

ISBN 1-929250-21-5

"Cake" was previously published in *In the Pillow Font*, Laguna Poets Series #165, by The Inevitable Press. "Blue Roses" has been previously published in *The Blue Mouse* by Swan Duckling Press.

Original cover art courtesy of the author.

Printed in Microsoft Optimum True Type

FarStarFire Press is devoted to providing a forum for uniquely sophisticated poets' voices. The Pale Ale Series is based on featured readers at the Thursday evening readings hosted by John Gardiner. Weekly readings are held at the Laguna Beach Brewing Company on Pacific Coast Highway, in Laguna Beach, California.

Table of Contents

My Trip to the L.A. County Museum of Art...	4
Cake	7
Haiku for the Master Electrician...	8
Violets in Cinema Haiku	9
Sequel to Cake	10
Poem That Resolves Itself...	11
Why I Hate Ancient Rome	13
The Naked One	14
How Do You Get the Raindrops to Stand Still	16
Imperfect Sonnet for Dialogue 13...	17
For the Punk on the Stairs in *Pretty in Pink*	18
Helvetica Has No Seraphs	19
Your Rapture or Mine?	21
Blue Roses	22
In the Sink	23
Home for Wayward Omens	24
Forgetting Ted Hughes	26
Semantics and the Word "Lover"	28
In My Mythology...	29
Considering the Lilies of the Field	30
My Brother Says This Is a Poem	32
Memory Poem #1	33
Found Poems	34
Memory Poem #2	35
Extra	36
The Wedding Poem	38

My Trip to the Los Angeles County Museum of Art
or
The Tar Pits Have Good Feng Shui

The Amarna Revolution did wonders for the kissability
of Egyptian lips
but there are rules here.
I don't care how cute the ears are,
you can't hug that princess's head
and
don't bite the carnelian.

I beg my friend to cause a distraction,
perhaps involving the Pharonic tweezers,
so I can climb up on that pedestal,
kneel down in front of that
six-foot-high statue of Akenaten's face
and find out what symmetry feels like.

It doesn't work.
We end up in the back room,
discovering that "Thoth" is a funny word and
listening to a stranger explain that she used to have
beads the color of that vase over there.
"They were round, "
she said
"and had holes for the string to go through."

I leave my friend in the bookstore
after he suggests that I buy
the cute little sarcophagus backpack.

At the Japan Pavilion,
the guard says, "Through the gold doors.
Start at the top,
and walk your way down."
At the top there are figures standing on lotuses,
in various states of favor granting gesture.
I am led down past the landscapes
by a Lucite railing
made from the distilled essence of palm trees on film.

At the bottom, there is an aggressively serene fountain.
The bottom is not the exit.
I push the wrong button in the elevator,
and wind up back at the lotuses again.
This reminds me of two things,
one of them, in reverse.

Tomorrow is an upside-down mobile,
and the gate
is the Smiths reference I've been trying to avoid.
My friend turns to me in the car and says,
"I know what the keys are,
but what is a yate?"
I cancel our date for the museum of miniatures,
break his tape deck,
and ask

"How long
have you had
to figure this out?"

Cake

She has ordered
one of those desserts
with the word "mountain" in its name
she's not even eating it, she's sculpting
as she forks a grid into the top blob of vanilla ice cream,
I distract myself with modernist word association:
Bauhaus, De Stijl, Jersey Shore hotels, red,
yellow, blue, no arches, no columns, no
ornament, no pointy roofs,
no cake, no cake, no cake.

People are telling stories, but I can't hear them
because every cell in my body has stopped
mid-mitosis,
evolved a larynx
and is shouting for unattainable hot fudge and frosting.
They're marching, chanting, rallying 'round the cause
Yelling "We want cake!"
          "We want cake!"

"Quiet, cells," I say
"We can't afford cake. We're saving up for
photocopies."
My cells believe that there is culture
at Kinko's
and so, when the Waiter asks
"Are you done with that?"
I let her say
Yes.

Haiku for the Master Electrician, Whose Job Title Sounds Omnipotent

When Tom leaves, he says,
"Blow out your candles, Laura."
You can't control that.

Violets in Cinema Haiku

Peckinpah rape scene
Row of frat boys laughs and cheers
Next week, Deliverance.

Sequel to Cake

The fork knows I end the night full,
and so do you.
When I signed up to become
a series of small sacraments
you lent me your pen
and were sure to point out
the White Mountain.

Our waitress is made of red drapes and comets and
SHE brings ME water and says thank you
and this kind of thing happens all the time.
We are saving ourselves every minute
with these lists of noticing.

The chair knows to sit me beneath you
you stroke my hair, tying the strings that bind angels
to Christmas trees.
Your hands
would ask nothing
of grateful mittens.

I conceal my sharp exhale
and lofty aspirations.
The alphabet soup in my veins
can't currently translate
oxygen,
only this,
and you, and yes, and home,
and not wanting, not wanting, so this
is not wanting,
and somewhere,
Fruition.

Poem That Resolves Itself While Listening to *Weezer's* Second Album; "Pinkerton"

Now that we've proven
that I can get what I want
and still have a story to tell,
and neither one of us has to rely on rejection
for inspiration,
at least not for the next couple of minutes,
the problem arises of how to take these precious little
snippets of intimacy,
obscure the details,
and turn them into public property.

Since this poem is the naked metal tip
of my red umbrella
held prone to the lightning bolts
of two very neurotic clouds,
now's a good time to bring out Zeus and Europa
who've been nagging me to put them in a poem
since last summer.
IF ANYONE turned into a bull
and dragged anyone ELSE to the middle of the ocean,
it was ME dragging YOU,
and when your feet got wet,
you turned, word for word,
into the *Blair Witch Project,* until I threatened you,
repeatedly,
with the ending of *Chasing Amy,*
Wherein the girl always wins.

Like movies,
numbers are a good way to distance oneself
from a potentially emotional situation.
So how about a list of facts that seem unrelated,
but are held together by the fact that I've numbered them,
and they all remind me of you:

1. Andy Warhol invented the word "Superstar". We don't know what they called them before that.

2. Someone once summed up his entire childhood for me, by saying this:
   "When I was four, it was dark."

3. All of my poems are about hunting and gathering. This one has more gathering.

But if you asked me to deconstruct this metaphorical wall of pillows,
to stop feeding you Joseph Campbell Soup
with a postmodern spoon,
this would be a very short poem,
and would come down to dancing
in the shower
and singing along
to *Weezer's* second album,
"Pinkerton".

Why I Hate Ancient Rome

Rome fell today. Good.
That's what they get
for building all those buildings
on top of each other.

The Romans stole
free-standing statues, melted them
and made copies
that couldn't be trusted
not to fall down.

In 313 A.D, the Romans
legalized
the concept
of inanimate objects.
Without them, we'd be Orthodox Etruscans.
These bad decisions
got more obnoxious
after electricity was invented.

Rome fell today. Good.
That's what they get
for building all those buildings
on top of each other.

The Naked One

The only pictures I have of Philadelphia
are unframed slides.
Assignments from lighting class.
I lift them gently from their gold box,
and press them to the window.

First is a noon-pink wrought iron railing.
Shadows reminding me how to think in terms
of F-stops, El trains, and negative spaces.

Next a black banister
covered in raindrops.
Did I tell you I used to photograph raindrops?
The rest are naked pictures of me.

In the first few, I face the camera and sit on my record
collection, shoulders straight, knees snapped shut, and
the way my blackberry lips snarl around that generic
cigarette says I'm nineteen, I'm naked, and I will never
believe a word you say. I am so uncompromisingly
selfish that I WILL interrupt the most important part of
what you're trying to tell me. The worst thing you can
do is shush me. The worst thing you can do, is ignore
me. I will be what you mean every time you say
Why do you have to keep
reminding me?

Me from above is the one you'd take home, take care
of, clean up after, and if she asked you to, you'd let her
sleep in your back seat and you would drive her
wherever it is she needs to go in life. She's the pretty
one because she looks so

careful.

Left hand cups left breast like it's a Minoan artifact or a
box of kittens, right hand pushes head toward shoulder
exposing neck;
this neck is the only thing about me that ever managed
to look

delicate

without simultaneously threatening to snap
like a chicken bone.

In the last one, I'm crouched in a corner like a *Cure*
video, and a silver whistle hangs from my wrist. Our
teacher interpreted the hunted baby animal look on my
face as movie star histrionics, said I'd make a fine little
fashion photographer someday, but I know that look
was real fear, like the real fear that you see

right now.

How Do You Get the Raindrops to Stand Still

1. Ample lighting and a fast shutter speed- otherwise, they'll look like lines.
2. Tell them they look pretty tonight.
3. Raindrops are very perceptive, so don't try to hide your neuroses, have endearing ones.
4. Erect a whole mythology around them, convincing them that it's destiny.
5. Accept the eventuality of puddles.
6. Listen.

Imperfect Sonnet for Dialogue 13 of Plato's Republic, Poetry and Unreality

To think that there must only be one bed
To think that bed of craftsman isn't real
On poetry, the lowest mind is fed
That Magritte's apple constitutes a meal

In Feeling lies the stupidest of Mind
and Knowledge, then, can never be complete
and Reason makes the only way to find
to look both ways before you cross the street

Restricted now to only hymns to gods
Reduced to paintings only modernistic
So take a crack at certain lightning rods
Assured that Plato finds you solipsistic

Catharsis has not place in Plato's Greece
Ionia doth spurn the hated id
A medicine the only way for peace
On Truths that aren't, one must put a lid

If darker parts be left to rust and die,
then Plato's truth, in Freud, becomes a lie.

P.S. I know Plato's not from Ionia,
    I used it because it's iambic.

For the Punk on the Stairs in *Pretty in Pink*

It's good to know
you were at every slumber party I ever had.

Between baking brownies
and Truth or Dare
between the folds of my Care Bears sleeping bag
between shivering
at the squeak of mating Barbie Dolls
and saying
"I wish there was a way to know what it feels like
 right now."

And you were there
in Philadelphia
when I could no longer stand the smell of the darkroom.

And when I was monochromatic
in the same hue, saturated
in glitter, and platinum, and sweat
you were there.

When the *Alpha Team* remix of the *Speed Racer* theme
song was spun at least 6 times a night in the clubs,
and when Superstar DJ Keoki remixed that remix
to include the sounds of cartoon orgasms,
you were there,
to draw a logarithmic spiral
beneath my right eye.

Why didn't you convince Molly
to make a better choice?
(lord knows it would be the first time.)

Helvetica Has No Seraphs

When I say "Trying to please the father,"
I mean my actual human father,
the stand-up comedian
in Rochester, New York,
and not "God the Father,"
because don't get me started
on the genders of deities.

My father claims he is too literal,
although he once said
"The worst thing that happened to me
during the tornado
was that I ran out of croutons"
then asked for how many things
can croutons be a metaphor?

My father is a neo-Seinfeldian.

During the Eighties, he named all of our pets
after Anne Tyler novels:
our dog was *Dinner at the Homesick Restaurant*
my pony, *The Accidental Tourist*.

Once, when my sister and I began cleaning our room
with an elaborate process of Barbie-grooming,
he walked in, saw the mess on the floor,
saw what we were doing and decreed that since we
couldn't take care of things, every toy,

down to the last broken crayon,
was to be locked in the attic
until the end of the World Series-
it wasn't even the playoffs yet.
Strawberry Shortcake was never heard from again.
Hello Kitty has no mouth.

In his absence,
I accumulate lots of little fathers.
For one of them, I wrote a 20-page paper
on the History of Graphic Design.

You wanna know about FONTS?
I can tell you about fonts.

Your Rapture or Mine?

1. I've been looking all over
for Bouguereau's painting of Cupid and Psyche
through every book of French 19th century everything.
I found them in her bathroom,
on a shelf above the litter box.
I visit them once a week,
and the four of us watch movies
always with the same plot:
someone is stuck, and then they move on.

2. She says "I have some good Spanish wine,
which I'd offer you, but I drank some last night,
then poured back the rest of the glass."
She doesn't realize that we are in a love poem,
and red wine, congealed by her saliva,
constitutes the perfect beverage.
I say "Not only will I drink it, but I will dab your
stigmata perfume on my wrists and sniff it proudly,
as though it were Chanel number 3.141592656,
et cetera.

    Then you can use the rest to dye my hair the color of
a Dionysian tampon.
I trust you.

3. Corinthians Chocolate Wafers?
Are you kidding me?
She has cleared my head
with Pentecostal cookies.

Blue Roses

1. When I was a little girl,
   afraid of the dark,
   my mother would sit by my bedside and sing
   for hours.
   One more song,
   please, just one more song.
   My mother knew the sounds of so many animals
   that by the time I finally drifted off to sleep
   she'd be e-i-e-i-ohing the sounds
   of extinct, flightless waterfowl,
   found only on the cave walls.
   This is what you are to me tonight.

2. With a piece of tinsel,
   stolen from a spider web, you trace
   the lines of my palm.
   "If I were to draw your hand,"
   you say
   "This is what it would look like.
   I would draw no contours.
   Only you would recognize these lines
   for what they are."

3. A Jungian Prayer:
   Let irony be poetic justice.
   Let Electra always be Electra.
   Let archetypes be beautiful.

4. Return of the Jedi.
   Resolution.
   Sleep.

In the Sink

I can tell by the way he flirts with me
that they have a stable relationship
that a well-placed pet name
or a kiss hello just close enough to real
won't make their world come crashing down.

She picks up his empty ice cream bowl
and she puts it in the sink.

I bought special pajamas for tonight
pink ones, with hearts
fearing that monkeys would be too cliché.
This is the danger of anticipation.

She picks up his empty ice cream bowl
and she puts it in the sink.

We just met,
but I've had a crush on him
for ten years.

She picks up his empty ice cream bowl
and she puts it in the sink.

To say "Someday I will find someone just like him"
is safer, and more likely
than having actual him.

In.
The.
Sink.

Home for Wayward Omens

Welcome.
Tread lightly.
Everything in this room is a talisman,
and the furniture is purely metaphorical.

Please excuse the appearance of the bedspread,
it used to be an outside blanket.
It once spread me in the lawn of a hysterical sunrise,
waking up the neighbors,
laughing at the fizzing sky.
Me and this blanket split a *Chipwich* at Lollapalooza 2.

You are standing on the stagnant chi
of too many library books
at once.

The clothes drying on the empty curtain rod
are used to more deciduous windows.

The photo albums are only recent,
the rest of the years cemented to the pillars and loos
of now-defunct coffee shops,
along with sacriliciously Exacto-ed comic books
belonging to former slaves.

I never took down the Christmas lights.
I never took down the Christmas cards.
I never took down the map of last month's
constellations.

I do not let go.

The dusty telescope reflects
my lack of perspective.

If I promise to be good this time,
will you stay?

Forgetting Ted Hughes

I thought the color of my lover's car
was rare and precious until I stood
waiting, watching the outbreak of highway
violets
as rampant as road rage.
Somebody else look for them now.
I only need one.

Echo

Only need one to cure the little white marshmallow
headaches framing my eyes
like who needs peripheral vision, anyway?

Echo

Peripheral vision, anyway, now's
no time to get devoted,
but what if I never see him
again?

Echo

See him again,
stop reading his lines instead of my own,
and for god's sake woman, learn to drive.

Echo

Learn to drive the lightning that he's woken up in me
It's mine now
and it need not see him as an outlet

Echo

See him as an outlet for a perpetual theme of
disappearing, repeating, explaining,
talking too much where no words are required

Echo

No words are required.

Semantics and the Word "Lover"

The first assignment:
(re)read the first ten pages
of the Lotus Sutra
bring me the flowers
that fall from the sky.

In My Mythology, Which, Admittedly, I Made Up, This Dream Means Change

Back there,
there is a field of blueberries
we never could find the end of
In the dream this is where
he held me hostage

A man who taught Graphic Design
as a Philosophy course is bending
toward my private parts
and barking
and it's not funny
because I can't escape

I say I have twenty houses
all in a row
all square
all mine to run through
but no one believes me when I
say help
this man is Blue Velveting me
There isn't safety
A verb is born.

Considering the Lilies of the Field

I came here for a long time
before I realized that Krishna is blue
she says
there are paintings of him all over the place
she says
I just never noticed

I tell her I wanted to dance so desperately today
enough to almost call old raver friends
enough to overcome
my terror of binary code
to risk spending too much
to miss a sunrise
because someone thinks it would be really cool
to leave right exactly at 4:20

Instead I am gently
foot to foot to temple floor
watching as the dancer in front of me
smiles not vacantly and reaches for paper ivy
tonight pebbles have been compared favorably to gold
foot to foot to knees to face the temple floor
before dinner we bow
to smell dancing on tiles
not yet evaporated

As an appetizer, we run our hands through flame
that's so nice of them
they think of everything
We are given gold Styrofoam plates,
and not one cup, but two
we are still
we are served
infinite amounts of saffron colored food
God is infinite amounts of saffron colored food
God mixes well with rice

We chose
to sit here
where the food is.

My Brother Says This Is a Poem
(On the Way to Philadelphia)

Oh, that's so sad.
A little dog dish on the side of the road.
Do you think it belongs to a coyote?

Memory Poem #1
(A Moon Poem)

1. Memory poems
   don't seem to be as effective
   as those which convey
   a sense of immediacy.
   My moon poems fall short
   from the decrease in gravity
   and lack of wind.

2. There is a locked door
   between me and the doorbells
   in my ex-girlfriend's apartment building.
   I used to think this was pretty stupid.

3. As I rounded this corner in a power outage,
   shielding her eucalyptus-scented candle,
   I noticed the important philosophical difference
   between candles that say "calm" on them
   and those which say "sensual."

4. We argued over which one of us was more holy.
   This argument is won by being the next
   to fall in love
   again.

Found Poems

Found Poem, Route 13 to Ithaca

open when flashing

Found Poem, Cincinnati Airport Bathroom

Automatic sink;
To turn water on\ stand in front of sink
To turn water off\ walk away from sink
Sink does not operate for black clothing.

Taoist Found Poem, San Diego Runway

use
minimum
thrust

Memory Poem #2
(A Meditation on Self-medication)

We have been given ecstasy
as a prescription to stop the crying.

Ecstasy makes you enlightened
like acid makes you smart.

Given to such shortcuts,
we sit on the gray carpet
folding paper cranes
out of gum wrappers and horoscopes.
Each time having no idea how we've done it.
Each time holding it in a flat hand to feel its weight.

In this way we learn the difference
between full of stars
and full with stars.

And note the musical nature
of the names of those who are gone.

Extra

I may look familiar.
I was in a movie once.
It was called *"Really Disturbing Behavioral Pattern
I'd Better Learn Myself Out Of."*
It had an all star cast of thousands.

I was Girl Crying in Airport With Flowers.
I was Girl With a Terminal Case of Optimistic Paranoia.
I was Girl Singing Ani Difranco Songs at Inappropriate
	Moments and Making Everyone Uncomfortable.
I was Girl Handing Out Light Until the Bulb Burns Out.

I had two lines,
both performed with hand Velcroed to forehead:

"I shall never love again"

and

"I have grown weary of accountability"

The movie is a cult classic
in certain small wooded areas of Eastern Europe.

Audiences know all of the dance numbers.
(Of COURSE there are dance numbers)

At the appointed times, they shout

"Live or die, but don't poison everything!"
and "Duh!" at the screen.

In theaters that allow it, audiences throw pancakes
and the dead kittens of childhood
each time I appear.

I have it on video,
on the shelf next to *Blue Velvet*
and *Breakfast at Tiffany's*
and they are all three, in essence,
the same movie.

The Wedding Poem

Begin with the sound of glass dashed against fireplace.

1. On my sister's would-be wedding day,
   she walked around
   with someone else's child on her hip.
   Grandpop has informed her
   that she has fallen behind her friends,
   in the reproducing department.
   He doesn't know that this is just that kind of town.

2. Silver is the color for weddings this year.
   There's a church across from my work,
   and on Saturdays,
   I watch the bizarre constellations
   of bridal photographs.
   She often looks like a ghost.

3. Rachel, my best friend, younger than me,
   has found a constructive outlet
   for her condescension.
   Her body has taken over,
   and babies make her cry.
   She has a backup plan,
   in case she never falls in love.
   We recognize
   unfair time constraints.

4. The neighborhood bar was quiet,
   until the matrimonial bar brawl.
   It begins with the bride arguing over the price
   of potato chips, and quickly degenerates
   to cummerbunds asunder.
   Rachel loses her seat as it becomes a weapon,
   and I gain the errant white sequins floating in my gin,
   torn from unrestrained elbows.
   The barkeep apologizes,
   Rachel fills out an application,
   and I stop looking for omens.
   The bride is still bleeding champagne
   from a closed bar.

5. This is the house I will marry myself out of:
   There are two cats named after Faith and Love.
   There are eight pillows on my bed.
   There are purple towels,
   and lavender scented soaps.
   Each day I boil myself in chlorine,
   wait for things I didn't want to want.

FarStarFire Press is proud to offer the following titles:

- *Upside Brown*: by Derrick Brown — Jan 1999
- *The Blue Book Poems*: by Carole Luther — Feb 1999
- *Traildust*: by John Gardiner — Mar 1999
- *Beaches Vol. 1 and Vol. 2*: by Bil Luther — Apr 1999
- *For Lori*: by Daniel McGinn — May 1999
- *Girltalk*: by Katya Giritsky — Jun 1999
- *The 1999 Laguna Beach, CA Slam Team* — Jul 1999
- *Borrowing Li Po's Moon*: by John C. Harrell — Aug 1999
- *Fruit On My Lips*: by J.D. Glasscock — Sep 1999
- *The Dark Beyond the Stars*: by Cassandra Hill — Oct 1999
- *Learning to Speak*: by Victor D. Infante — Nov 1999
- *You Make the Balloons, I'll Blow Them Up*: by Paul Suntup — Dec 1999
- *Two Sides Now*: by Misty Mallory & Lee Mallory — Dec 25, 1999
- *Scream!*: by Bil Luther — Jan 2000
- *Season of the River*: by Lawrence Schulz — Feb 2000
- *Trusting the Moon*: by John Gardiner — Mar 2000
- *Stuck in the Middle*: by Jaimes Palacio — Apr 2000
- *64 Crayons*: by Carole Luther — May 2000
- *Laguna Beach, CA Slam Team 2000* — Jun 2000
- *Homesick for Heaven*: by Catherine Spear — Jul 2000

Future Publications to Include:

- The Tao Te Ch'ang: a multimedia CD by Jim Fontana, Bil Luther and Carole Luther.
- Twenty Years: a multimedia CD version of John C. Harrell's print work with Moki Martin, artist.
- Tao and Zen Wilderness: a multimedia CD by John Gardiner, Carole and Bil Luther.

FarStarFire Press
26701 Quail Creek, Suite 251
Laguna Hills, CA 92656
949.362.7499
http://www.farstarfire.com